My Story

By Nuha Sifri Zakharia

My Story

29 November 2009

By Nuha Sifri Zakharia

I was born in Jaffa, Palestine. At that time, Palestine was ruled by the British Mandate. The mandate began in the year 1917 and ended in the year 1948. The Belfor Declaration issued in 1917 by Lord Belfor, the Foreign Minister of Great Britain, comprised a promise to render Israel a homeland in Palestine thus, encouraging the Israelis to migrate to Palestine illegally. Consequently, since the establishment of the State of Israel in 1948, conflict in the Middle East had been a persistent threat to the region in particular and the world in general.

Now back to my biography, I was raised up with three other children by conservative parents. My mother was an educated woman as well as my father.

I received my Elementary and Secondary education at schools in Jaffa, followed by the London Matriculation Degree. After graduation, I was appointed a teacher at Tabeetha Mission School which was close to where I lived. Our rented spacious apartment was on the second floor in a building sited in Faisal Street in Jaffa. The region was populated by a sophisticated community comprising both Christians and Muslims of decent descents.

As a teenager, I was attractive, slim and tall. A number of young men asked for my hand, of course from my father. As familiar, we have our own culture and traditions, whereas we were allowed to meet the bridegroom only after the father's approval in coordination with the bride. To make the story brief, I was introduced to a young man whom my father was convinced of, and shortly after, I was engaged to him. At that time, I was working as a teacher just newly appointed. The bridegroom was living in Jerusalem. He used to visit us once per week, on his week ends. I have tried to like my fiancé, but unfortunately, there was no compatibility between him and myself, though he was good looking and of a good family. I told my father about my negative feelings towards that young man, but my father never listened to me. Therefore, one day I decided to break up the engagement. I discussed it with my mother who eventually supported my feelings and suggested to leave with her all the gifts which the bridegroom had given me on several occasions. I remember I did what she said to me and left to school. During my absence she explained everything to my father who showed anger and rage, but unwillingly met the brother of my fiancé and gave him all the gifts and apologized for the bad luck. The brother, who was a doctor, was the superintendent of the French Hospital in Jaffa.

On the afternoon of that day, I returned back from school to find my father so furious. I went straight to my room. My mother followed and told me that my father was very angry and that I have to be very calm. I did that. We had a long discussion and everything went along peacefully, but at the end he said that he shall never interfere with my marriage, and that he is not my father and me not his daughter. He said that in an angry manner still rejecting the idea of breaking the engagement. Before going any further, it is worth mentioning that I met my fiancé again after seventeen years. I was married and was visiting my seventeen years old daughter who was studying at the Beirut College for women BCW in Beirut Lebanon. On my way back to Amman, Jordan, to visit my mother, I boarded the plane (Middle East Airlines) and to my surprise, I met my fiancé who sat next to me. He was surprised and said "what a small world to meet again".

We spoke about the past and how I rejected him. He was married to a friend of mine from Jaffa. He invited me to visit them at home in Amman. However, we departed at Amman airport and had never seen him again.

I loved my father and was proud of him. He had a very strong personality and respected by all who knew him. Despite what he uttered about his involvement re- my marriage, he still was the man of the house decision wise.

Now that the burden is off my shoulder, I was a real happy teenager. I proceeded with my work at school never thinking of anyone at all.

1948 – My parents Victoria and Issa Sifri in Jaffa

Shortly after, a number of young men proposed especially when they heard about my breaking of the engagement. My father, being responsible for his home affairs including his children discussed the subject with me in the presence of my mother and the rest of family members. Also during the same period, it happened that while I was going out of school, a new proposal saw me and inquired about me. He was driving his own private car. He asked his niece who was teaching at the same school about me, and the latter gave him all the information she is familiar of. Also, he asked her to arrange for a teacher's party to be held at her house and that she did. Though, at first I have declined to go but another teacher who was a close friend of mine insisted that I should go. Unknowing what is going on, I participated. All teachers gathered there in the formal sitting room including the proposal who is the teacher's uncle, also her married sister and husband. As usual everybody was talking and joking including myself, and while I was looking around, I discovered that the new future bridegroom kept looking at me to an extent that I was so bashful and stopped talking or joking or laughing. The second day, the new bridegroom met with his family, and arranged to meet my father to ask for my hand. This they did and the engagement day was set, but of course, after meeting the new bridegroom in a gathering planned by relatives. (To our surprise, we came to know during that gathering, that my mother and the bridegroom were both graduates of the Bishop school (St. Mary's for Girls, and St George's for Boys) in Jerusalem.

The engagement day took place on 23/2/1947 in our house. We kept engaged for two months. On 23/05/1947, the wedding was celebrated at St George's Greek Orthodox Church in Jaffa followed by a reception in an adjacent hall belonging to the Church.

Soon after, we got ready to go for our honey moon. In his own private car, my husband drove all the way along the coast to Beirut Lebanon. There we stayed at Regent Hotel. We spent one whole week in Beirut, and then proceeded to Syria. On our way to Damascus, we passed by Al-Biqua, a beautiful resort, and stayed there for two nights.

1947 – Our wedding at St George's Greek Orthodox Church in Jaffa

During our stay in the hotel, we called our parents in Jaffa. My father picked up the phone and asked about us, and then my mother, who had a short chat with us, informed me about the death of my grandmother right after our departure.

It was really unexpected to hear the sad news. I loved my grandmother so much and it took me a while to get over it.

1947 – Our Honeymoon in Syria

After spending few days in Al-Biqua', Lebanon, we proceeded in our private car to Damascus, Syria. We spent there two weeks. We toured the city which has its own heritage, and visited historical places. I remember we had ice-cream in one of its famous markets.

Now that our honey moon had ended, we started packing. In this regard, I would like to mention that during our stay in Beirut and Damascus, we bought a number of items including runners for our dining table, end tables, and coffee table etc. The Venetian embroidered runners were hand made and expensive. They match the beautiful furniture my husband had provided before the wedding, its worth to say that I had an elegant home at Faisal Street in Jaffa. We left Damascus to Beirut in our car. We stayed two days at the hotel and then headed to Jaffa, back to our new furnished home. The rent of that apartment was really high, but because it was located near my parent's home, my husband rented it for my own sake to be near my family.

I was so close to my parents. I used to visit them nearly every day and they did the same by stopping by in the morning especially my father before he goes to work. I had no experience in cooking, and therefore, my mother used to help and direct. After a month since my wedding, I became pregnant. My parents and my husband were happy to hear the good news. During the nine period of pregnancy, my mother and I were preparing what is needed for a child ie. winter and summer clothing. I remember the beautiful hand knitted baby sweaters, dresses, jerseys "berbatose" it is a French word, coats etc. of various soft baby wool color which were knitted by a specialized hand knitting worker called Mary living across our apartment at King Faisal Street. She knitted all the baby wool items needed for the coming baby to be born. In other words, the baby had already a beautiful trousseau, a pram, a bed etc. During the first three months of my pregnancy, I had morning sickness. It reminds me of having same symptoms while I was at church (the Greek Orthodox Church in Jaffa), whereas, my mother was obliged to leave church to escort me with my husband to our private car which was parking in the compound of the church. After resting for a while, we three went back to join the congregation. However, soon after the morning sickness disappeared, my mother who lived right next to my apartment started to train me on cooking etc. Also, during the same period, the conflict between the Arabs and Jews under the rule of the British mandate was uprising. Sometimes, it was really scary and dangerous.

At that time, I had a servant named Nimer. He used to assist in my house work especially carrying the food which my mother used to cook. At that time I had no experience in cooking; it is ridiculous, isn't it? Actually, I had a wonderful time - good parents, wonderful husband and a beautiful home and environment. Moreover, we had nearly everyday visitors to congratulate the marriage bringing with them valuable gifts, which, of course, we will return on occasions such as ours.

Being near my parents, I used to visit them nearly everyday, and they did likewise. My father was a prominent writer author and a poet. He used to write political articles in the news papers published in Jaffa criticizing the British Mandate re- their unfair policy towards the Palestinians by stealing their land and because of that he was once imprisoned in a concentration camp in Acre, a small city North of Palestine for a whole year as a punishment. We were young and my mother tried her best to release him by meeting the British District Commissioner General in Jaffa, who after her appeal released my father on the assumption that he can write articles that should abide to their policy and not against it. When I was young I still remember the sound of the boots of the British soldiers stepping the stairs up to the second floor to search our home especially the room/office of my father. Such surprise visits were made twice or thrice per month.

My father was an owner of a stationery and printing store. He wrote a number of books, all pertaining to the Arab/Israeli conflict, which were printed in his store, and it is worth to mention that copies of all the political books which my father had written can be found in the libraries of the Arab Universities in the Middle East. My father also owned a building with two floors built in Faisal Street as well. He planned to rent the first floor and live on the second floor with his family, but sad enough to say that he never did and this will be explained while narrating the tragic events happening all through the journey of my life.

As for my husband, he owned a pharmacy and drug store. He also owned a complex which comprised a number of rooms for rent. That complex was on the borders between Jaffa and Tel-Aviv. It was blocking the scene behind the building, thus forcing the Jews to demolish it completely in order to move forward with their fight with the unarmed Palestinians. Conflicts between the Arabs and Jews continued. There were daily casualties on both sides. Curfew was often imposed by the British mandate in the Palestinian sector in order to calm the situation. The inhabitants began to suffer emotionally and financially due to continuous instability and escalating conflicts between both parties. People wondered what to do. Some had decided to leave the country before the situation deteriorates. We were really scared especially after the battle which took place at Deir Yasseen village where as alleged; the Jews murdered the majority of its inhabitants. It was a heinous act of human massacre.

My father, and as previously mentioned, was a nationalist, so sincere to his country. His advice to his children and to himself was never ever leave our country. That was his decision, and we all counted on him and followed his footsteps, but the general political situation began to escalate to a scary direction night and day, thus not allowing the residents get a quiet sleep. On

April 1st, 1948, we had our first born baby whom we named Rima. She was an adorable beautiful child. Naturally, my mother was with me as well as the servant Nimer. They both took care of the house, cooking and the making of "moughli" which is a traditional formal sweet recipe to be offered to the congratulating relatives and friends who usually come with their gifts to say "mabrouk". On that day of April the 1st, rain was pouring and Spring began, but it was a spring of war! My father used to visit me every morning to see the innocent baby Rima in her cute bed staring at us with her blue eyes. She was a real pleasure to everyone, and a precious gift from God. Our baby kept me busy all day long. On the fifth of May 1948, the British Mandate over Palestine ended leaving the whole troubled country in the hands of the Israeli armed men and women called the Haganah!

The situation in Jaffa, because of the continuous conflict between the Palestinians and the Jews was tense. The majority of the people residing in Jaffa in particular and Palestine in general were leading an unstable daily life of fear. The idea of leaving the country was on the mind of every individual, but at the same time it was difficult to leave home, property and business, though we thought that our departure from our country will be just for a short period and not eternal.

The circumstances escalated and the Israeli army began bombarding the city of Jaffa and other places in Palestine with mortar bombs and air raids. Many were killed or injured. As for ourselves we left our home meaning my husband and our baby and took refuge in a relative house at Al-Ajami Quarter where at that moment it was safer than Faisal Street where our home is located. While hiding we heard the planes air raiding over where we were. My husband who was holding Rima bent down to protect the baby. At this point we decided to leave Jaffa in our own private car leaving everything behind us. My married sister with two daughters and husband living at Al-Ajami area also joined us leaving behind us our parents. It was really a very sad and detrimental moments to bid goodbye to our parents, hugging them and handing them the keys of our homes, believing that we will be back during a fortnight's period. With tears in our eyes we headed to an unknown destination just to escape the chaos, disaster and death, taking with us the only clothes we were wearing, and the little money we were keeping. I sat in the back seat with my only one-month old baby whom I was nursing, and next to me my sister with her two young daughters. My husband was the driver and my sister's husband sat next to him. After driving for an hour we passed by an Israeli settlement named (naiter).

To my knowledge, this settlement was a place for training (vocational training) and we used to pass by it when driving out of Jaffa during the rule of the British Mandate. But this time and unexpectedly, we were confronted by Israeli soldiers or Haganah, heavily armed and greeting us with a sarcastic and mocking smile while the snipers were behind them shooting at the escaping cars. Many were killed or wounded. As for us we were lucky to stay alive. We proceeded driving till we reached Ramallah. We spent one night there in a relative's house, and the second day we headed to Jordan. My sister and family hired another car and proceeded to Lebanon.

After a long tiring trip we arrived to Amman Jordan. Amman, the capital of Jordan, was a primitive, dirty and uncivilized country. The majority of the homes were made of mud or cheap construction, and despite of that the rents of the "shelters" were high!!!

My sister in law who migrated before us had rented a small room in Amman. She was living with her family and knowing that we were looking for refuge, she invited us to stay with them until the political situation clears up and we did. We stayed together with that nice family until my parents whom we had left in Jaffa were convinced by a relative to leave Jaffa immediately, lest the Jews might arrest my father being a political figure in Palestine. We left Amman to Salt where my parents where staying. The Bisharat family in Salt offered my parents their home as a temporary accommodation until our return to our homeland Palestine.

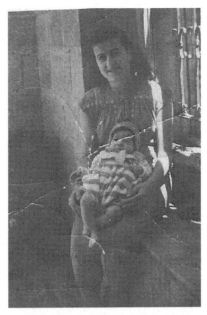

1948 – My daughter Rima with my sister Dumia in Salt

My father who was so determined not to leave his home in Jaffa was forced to leave unwillingly, carrying the keys of his home as well as those of his daughter's homes, also the keys of his store, and accompanied by my mother, said goodbye to Jaffa and had never returned. He migrated in 1948 and died in 1950 at the age of 53 due to a heart attack caused by grief, devastation and melancholy.

We all stayed together, my brother, my sister, my parents, my husband, our baby and I. It was so detrimental to each one of us to see ourselves in another country, leaving our properties, businesses and belongings behind us predicting and hoping that one day we will be going back to Jaffa. My father who was so well known and popular was so much disturbed and worried re-the situation, listening daily to the radio news, meeting with Palestinian refugees at the Bisharat unit. Talking about politics and other subjects re-our future and the future of the Palestinians who were driven out and scattered all over the Arab region. He was a prophet predicting the circumstances which will be taking place in the long run and that he had the feeling that the Palestinian refugees will never go back to their homes and that Israel will take over Palestine, looting homes and confiscating properties and lands etc. Time went on without any tangible solutions; my father, ourselves and the majority of the Palestinian refugees went out of money. No work, no income and over and above we were supposed to pay the rent of the accommodation or shelters which the Jordanians had given to us and other Palestinian refugees in Salt or Amman or anywhere else.

We stayed in Salt with my parents for two months, sleeping on mattresses on the floor. The mattresses were brought by my parents in addition to few households which they have carried with them in the truck when they left Jaffa. As for the baby, we made a sort of a hammock for her to sleep in. The Bisharat family gave us few seats to use and a small table as far as I can remember. It was sad and frustrating to lead such a life with no hope ahead. Milk for feeding the baby was purchased from Amman (KLIM). My husband used to go to Amman by bus, buy a number of cans and return home. Fresh cow milk in Salt is dirty. From the window where we were living on the second floor, I could see the owner of a small shop sifting the milk with a sieve!!! in order to pick the dead floating flies. Incredible

ANOTHER PHASE

Now my husband began thinking of going back to a town named Ashkelon in Israel to be close to Jaffa and to be near his brother who is his partner in the pharmacy business. I rejected the idea and started crying saying that I will never ever leave my parents being my self young with a two months old child. My father, who was rather strict, said that I should go with my husband wherever he wants. Again I said no and my mother took my side and defended me and was completely against my father. To make the story short, my father won and I was obliged to take my baby and together with my husband travelled to Ashkelon via an illegal method of transportation. It was risky and scary especially with an infant. I cried and cried and cried all through the way until we arrived to Ashkelon leaving my family behind me and my father whom I never saw again after my departure. He died in 1950.

On arrival we were greeted by my brother in law, his young kids, their mother, her brother and father. They were surprised how we could make it to travel that entire long tiring trip via illegal dangerous routes and with a baby to their home.

However, we were welcomed, and my sister in law provided me with fresh clean cow milk to feed our baby. In this respect, I forgot to mentioned, that I was breast feeding my baby, but due to panic and calamities, I lost my milk and that is why we fed her with KLIM formula and when we ran out of it, as mentioned above, my sister in law provided me with clean nutritious fresh cow's milk.

The first question my sister in law asked is why did we leave our home in Jaffa, and that it was a big mistake for the Palestinians to leave their country and go to no where leaving behind all what they have established all through their life. Also she added that in her case, whatever happens she would never ever think of leaving her home to be confronted with sufferings and devastations, and, my answer to her was that the Palestinians were driven unwillingly from their homes due to the continuous Israeli air raids, mortar bombs over residential areas, towns and villages. However, my sister in law and family had followed our steps when Ashkelon was completely destroyed by the savage Israeli air raids, they migrated to the US.

My brother in law was a Pharmacist, his wife used to help him and look after home and two kids a boy and a girl. We were leading a day by day life, counting the days and looking forward to hear the good news to go back to our home and city. But that never happened. It was the turn of the town of Ashkelon to be ruined and the Palestinian residents to be killed or to be driven out of their homes similar to what had taken place in other cities towns and villages in Palestine. One night around 10pm, we were awakened up by the sound of explosions and noise of Israeli war planes roaming the skies of Ashkelon. My brother in law and his wife suggested that we leave the house and hide under the trees of an orange grove near by in order to avoid disaster or death. We immediately, and still in night gowns, we wrapped our two months old sleeping baby, grabbed her bottle, milk, small burner (to warm the milk) and the used old pram (once used by my sister in law when raising her children) and rushed out on foot to the nearby orange grove and hid under the orange trees. We kept distances between us ie. me and baby under one tree, my husband under another tree, my sister in law and kids under a far away tree and so on. This was planned in order to allow

18

those who stay alive to rescue the injured or dead. I still remember the wicked noise of the war planes circling around over the town of Ashkelon. We were all breathless awaiting our disaster and expecting anytime the descending of bombs over the orange grove where we were hiding. I was shivering due to cold and fear. The baby cried she was hungry. The milk was cold. I have tried to warm it by turning on the small burner which my sister in law had given me, and of course I have to use a match to operate it. The people hiding all over the orange grove, families and others, shouted at me forbidding me to light the small burner lest the war planes would see the spark! Of course I was obliged to feed the baby cold milk, which she had rejected and kept crying. The hiders kept yelling at me saying that I should shut up the baby's mouth and prevent her from crying which I could not be able to do it despite my continuous efforts to calm the baby. We were all devastated, no nerves no patience, but fear and death. The Israeli planes threw missiles all over Ashkelon haphazardly killing people and demolishing structures, homes and buildings. Hundreds of persons were killed or wounded. While still in the orange grove, we decided to leave the grove and hide in another safer site. I remember that the whole group took refuge in an old barn which we thought it would be far away from the sight of the war planes, and of course the three of us were among the group. We spent the night there, and I remember that our two months old baby could not sleep due to the bugs which were creeping in to her tiny body sucking her blood. I immediately changed her clothes and did what I could to prevent their creeping amongst the clothes of the innocent defend less creature. The baby never slept that fearful night. The whole group stayed awake waiting for an unknown future. While in that state of uncertainty, the war planes came back. My husband and I decided to leave the place and hide under one of the trees far away from the barn site. At the same time, I was preparing our baby's milk bottle. It was hot to feed the baby right away. Therefore, I wrapped her with a thick blanket, gave the bottle to my husband and rushed outside the place to hide under a big tree. It was extremely cold. We were shivering due to cold and panic. The milk bottle turned cold. The crying hungry baby rejected the bottle for being cold. My husband hid it under his clothes close to his chest to keep it warm, but his body added coldness to the milk due to fear. The war planes kept roaring and roaming over the area for a while. We were dead silent and the baby never stopped crying to be fed. Finally, the war planes dropped its load of explosions half a mile from where we were. My husband and I screamed loudly due to panic bending on our baby to protect her from harm. Her crying for food never stopped during the whole ordeal, but stopped when hearing the explosion and our screams!!! We prayed and thanked God for keeping us alive. We figured that tons of explosions were dropped over us, since the heavy smoke and sound were beyond description and we thought that were killed. Covered with dark smoke, debris and sand, devastated, sick and deaf, we grabbed our baby and rushed back to where we were at dragging inside to make another bottle. Thinking what to do, my husband thought of borrowing his brother's car to escape to Gaza. My brother in law reluctantly agreed to give the car to my husband alerting him at the same time to be cautious. With the few clothes we had and the baby's food, we headed to the Gaza strip. Having my baby sleeping on my lap, I could see the metal roof of the car bends down every time a mortar bomb passes over our heads from the Israeli side to the Egyptian side. .My husband got aware and found himself trapped in a most dangerous area. An Egyptian soldier who was hiding told us that the bridge between Ashkelon and Gaza has been knocked down by the Israelis, thus disconnecting Gaza Strip from Ashkelon and preventing the Egyptians from escaping. We immediately drove back to Ashkelon amid the flying mortar bombs above our heads.

Desperate, fatigue and panic with a two months old baby who needed diaper change food and sleep. My husband thought of spending sometime in the house of an old lady who lives in her own orange grove far away from where we were. The owner is the mother in law of my husband's sister. To make the story brief, we headed to that destination by car. The old lady named (Im Qustandi) was so pleased to see us and was so hospitable during our stay there. She provided me with fresh milk to feed our baby, food and comfortable lodging. We relaxed there for a while thinking what to do and where to go and at the same time giving space to the family of my brother in law since everyone was under severe tense not knowing what will happen the second day. The situation was dangerous and my husband thought of escaping to Gaza on a camel which at that moment was the only mean of transportation. Also going back to Jordan (Salt) to re-join my family via the same illegal way which we have unfortunately used when going to Ashkelon, had been blocked by the fighting parties and it was an adventure to go back. Therefore, the only out let is to ride on a camel to escape to Gaza.

To hire a camel led by its owner was expensive, since nearly all residents of Ashkelon wanted to run away to evade the Israeli air raids which were detrimental to every soul!!! I myself suffered pschychological symptoms - No sleeping, not eating, crying and horrified by the noise of the war planes which accompanied me night and day and for almost years...I became almost hysteric, but not forgetting my duties towards the innocent child which I did to the best of my abilities.

My husband and the owner of the camel reached to an agreement to how much the one way to Gaza would cost. I do not remember what the amount to be paid to the owner was. It was the first time in my life to ride a camel with my baby. The owner helped me to jump up and sit behind the hump of the camel. I got seated on an old throw and after adjusting myself well on the back of the camel, I was given my child whom I grabbed and held her tightly in my arms. My husband had no room and was obliged to walk all through the way to Gaza on foot on sandy area keeping one of his arms up towards me and the baby lest we may fall down especially when the camel occasionally had to bend down to reach grass or plants or other things to eat. I remember I use to scream whenever the camel bent to eat. It was a scream of devastation and fear and despair. My tears never dried!!!

1948 – with my daughter Rima in Gaza

After travelling for almost four hours through an illegal destination surrounded by sand and bushes and escorted by Israeli warplanes maneuvering the area, we reached our destination which was Gaza, (the Gaza Strip). The camel kept walking us to the house of a relative named Im Khalil Zakharia (Im means mother). She is a relative to my husband. She was a widow living with her two grown up sons and grown up daughter under one roof in the Zeitun area of Gaza. We were warmly greeted by her and her children. Their home comprised of three rooms. One room for her and her daughter, the second room for her two sons, while the third is named (salon) was for friends who sit there while visiting. It is usually kept tidy and clean. The salon room was given to us temporarily until knowing our future whereabouts. Living with this family was the grand daughter of Im Khalil and her name was Nawal.

Nawal was thirteen years old. The girl was pretty but mentally disabled. In order to assist her married daughter who lived in Jericho with her family Im Khalil took the responsibility of raising the grand daughter in her house for ever, thus rendering help and peace to the married daughter who had other three children. In fact the second unmarried daughter of Im Khalil who was a school teacher cooperated with her mother on daily basis to raise the sick grand daughter.

As I previously stated we were warmly received by the whole family. We spent the first night talking about our eviction from Jaffa followed by the calamities we have encountered thereafter. Naturally, I gave my baby a bath, fed her and put her to bed. We were really so tired and exhausted. I went to bed with tears in my eyes, and I wept quietly until I went into a deep sleep. I woke up early to change diapers and feed my beautiful daughter. I felt lost and devastated. I missed my parents and without exaggeration my tears never dried all through our stay in that house in the Zeitun Quarter

It was my first visit to Gaza. The British Mandate considered Gaza a place to exile personalities who were against the policy of the British rule. The town as far as I can remember was gloomy, dark and below the standard of civilization. The women, Christian and Muslims covered their heads and faces with black thick veils and wore black long gowns. To compare it to Jaffa where I was raised, there was no comparison whatsoever. I felt so depressed especially when I was obliged to cover my face during the first phase of my living there. At the same time the thought of joining my family in Salt was always on my mind. I was just surviving and living my day after day with the hope that I shall one day be re-united with my parents. But it never happened. I was yearning to go back to my home in Jaffa, but the thought of going back started to fade away, and the thought of going to Jordan had replaced it. We stayed with the Zakharia family for two months. They were so nice to us. Nawal, the mentally disabled girl was my concern in that house. Being myself sad and devastated, yet I have tried my best to keep an eye on Nawal lest she might hurt my daughter one day, and which unfortunately it did happen. I will write about this incident later in this book while narrating the sad biography of my life.

My husband and myself thought of moving out, just to give space to this nice family. We rented a one room only with an outside old fashioned toilet. The environment is below standard, very primitive inhabitants, poor dirty and the area was called Al-fawakheer. The word Al-fawakheer, means clay. The occupation of the people was to make jars pitchers, etc. out of clay which they burn finally on black coal. We rented in that poor area because it was cheap and actually we ran out of money. I cannot describe the depression I went through when I moved to that miserable shelter with a three months old child. We had nothing except a mattress and a small burner which we got from Im Khalil in addition to other limited miscellaneous things for our daily usage. We spent the first night and tried to get organized in that poor shelter. My priority was my baby, thus keeping her clean and well fed. Otherwise, I was constantly praying to God to re-unite me with my parents in Jordan. That was unfortunately my only hope at that time, and the single thought of returning back to Jaffa has been dropped for ever!!!

Living in that one single room was so hard and humiliating specially the environment. One night, as far as I can remember, while we were sleeping on the mattress on the floor, with the baby between us, I heard commotion outside the door and someone trying to open the door. It was around midnight, and I could see the handle of the wooden door going up and down. I was scared and slowly and silently tried to wake up my husband. He woke up and saw the handle of the door moving and pushing the door to open. Of course the door was locked from inside. My husband and myself just watched the action and were breathless from fear. We kept listening and watching until the thief ran away. We stayed awake with wide open eyes until morning light. Early next morning we opened the door and we could sea the traces of the feet of the thief climbing up to the roof of the room. The traces of the feet were black on a white wall. My husband called the police, and the latter said that the thief was from the poor fawakheer area because of traces of his black foot steps.

The Israeli air raids followed us to Gaza. Nearly every night, there was an air raid. In order to protect ourselves, we used to hide in a strong built house owned by the Tarazi family. Nearly every night we wrapped our baby with a thick blanket (since it was winter season) and walked on foot to that fortified house which was not so far from where we were living. Trembling and shivering all through the way, I could not wait to see myself reaching the house of that wonderful family who embraced us with love and care. Every individual of that family tried to ease the panic I went through. It was detrimental to me to hear the horrible sound of the war planes roaming above Gaza and above the Zeitoun area where we were hiding with other families including Im Khalil's family whom I was so glad to see. The sound of the planes tore me apart since I had enough zziiiiiiiin in my ears all through my migration from Jaffa, Ashkelon and then Gaza, and enough is enough. One night the war planes dropped their heavy weight of explosions on the poor densely populated area of Zeitoun where we were hiding. It was pretty close to our strong wide wall built building consisting of two floors. Around thirty human beings were taking shelter in that ancient strongly built house. I remember I could feel the density and heaviness of the bombs dropped over us as if heaven by itself fell over the earth!!! Something incredible and the panic we went through was beyond description. I was holding my baby trying to protect her. She started crying as if she knew what was happening. She did not stop crying until one of the girls there provided the milk bottle and fed her. I was totally devastated and desperate. Being with that group of nice people I felt somehow safe but defeated unknowing what the future is hiding for us. We spent the night in that house, and early next morning we walked on foot to the Fawakheer area to our miserable rented room carrying our sleeping five months old baby. The war planes kept air raiding Gaza for almost a month. Many people were killed or injured. After cease

27

fire announced by the UN. Our daily strolling on foot to the Tarazi house seeking security stopped. Now back to the poorly built rented room, we tried again to find a way to leave Gaza and go to Salt, Jordan to join my parents. But unfortunately, the political situation became more complicated and the illegal routes to Jordan got more dangerous, thus had no alternative but to stay in Gaza. We became short of money and asked Im Khalil if we can stay in her house for another month or more until we find a way to get money from my parents or relatives. Im Khalil and children welcomed our return and gave us a room in their newly rented house in Rimal Quarter which was a far better environment than the old house. In that house we were provided with a bed wide enough for three. Also, a small cupboard, table and a chair. Getting somewhat organized, we stayed with this hospitable family for a period of time. Naturally, I participated in the house work, helping the old lady in the kitchen work as well as cooking.

As mentioned before, the old lady was raising her 13 years old grand daughter who was mentally disabled. Her name was Nawal. I was, as usual, very attentive to my baby daughter less she may hurt her. Nawal was a non stop walking person exploring every corner of the house causing destruction and troubles. In other words, she was a trouble maker. The children of Im Khalil were against the idea of keeping her at home guarded by her grandmother and aunt. One day they discussed with their mother the idea of moving her to a mental hospital in Cairo Egypt, and that is not their responsibility to raise her up in their house while her parents are still alive. But their mother rejected the plan completely saying that it is her right to help her daughter by keeping Nawal in her care. The grand daughter was very well cared after by the grandmother. The latter used to feed her breakfast, dinner, and supper in addition to other eatable things. Her aunt, the teacher, used to take her for walks after work. The grandmother and granddaughter slept together in one wide bed. Every night and before going to bed Nawal was given a cup of chamomile to drink in order to keep her calm and quiet. Also during the day over and above what she ate, her grandmother used to give her the brain of the sheep after cooking it believing that it will help to enhance the growth of her damaged brains. The brains were affected after Nawal ran high fever as stated by her grandmother.

We stayed with that family, free board and lodging for four months. Every individual was extremely nice to us. Our daughter turned eight months. She was a healthy pretty baby with blue eyes and blond hair. As I may have mentioned before, I used to help the old lady in the kitchen work and take care of my daughter by keeping an eye on Nawal lest she might, God forbids, hurt my child. This was the advice of the old lady to me. While our daily life went on, including going out for walks, pushing the stroller of my daughter and thinking of my future destiny in this strange town separated from my parents, relatives and people whom I knew. My husband used to spend some time with the two sons of Im Khalil who owned a shop for spare parts in Gaza. My husband was jobless and short of money. The used stroller was given to us by friends of the old lady. It is heart breaking to remember my beautifully furnished home in Jaffa, and the elegant baby's pram and stroller, the baby's bed with its rich bedding and canopy, her clothes, etc.. I used to cry daily and my tears never stopped.

I am by nature very particular and organized. One day while putting away my husband's suit, it is my habit to search the pockets and clean them from dust. While I was going through that job, I found a short letter in one of the pockets written by my brother informing us about the death of my dear father. Obviously, it was sent by someone who came from Salt to Gaza. My husband, who knows how much I was so close to my parents hid the letter and kept the sad news to himself only. After reading it, I couldn't believe what I was reading and started crying unknowing what to do and how to behave. It was detrimental, a shock and a blow to all my dreams. I lost hope, and became so depressed and isolated. I could not reach my family since there was no communication whatsoever. We were in a state of war, misery and over and above the death of my beloved father. He died due to grief re-the eviction of the Palestinians from their country leaving behind rich homes and stores. He did not care for his properties or business as much as he cared for the devastating tragedy of the Palestinians fate who were scattered all over the Arab world. He died due a heart attack at the age of 53.

I loved my father and I was proud of him. Though, he insisted that I should join my husband through the trip to Ashkelon, and that after hearing what I have went through via my letters to him he regretted the decision he made and kept thinking of me and sending me letters and money to calm me down. My sufferings added stress and sadness to my beloved parents, and it was another factor in causing the fatal heart attack which my father had sustained while working as an editor to a Palestinian news paper in Amman owned by a Palestinian man who was a friend of my father when living in Jaffa Palestine. My father accepted the job just to keep him busy until his return to his home town Jaffa. It was a dream!!! Only a dream.

His death was a blow to the Arab world. Radios announced his death by saying that the Arab world has lost one of its prominent personalities. He struggled hard through his writings to awake the Arabs re- the danger of Zionism and how the British Government assisted the Jews to confiscate the lands and occupy the country as a whole.

I was in real grief, lost weight and only for my innocent child, I decided to survive by eating and drinking, or otherwise I became so desperate and depressed and had preferred death on life. The old lady was a great comfort to me. She condoled me by saying that this is God's will and that it is the destiny of the Palestinian people to suffer and go through all those calamities and loss. She also advised me to take care of myself and child and to lead normal life until one day we hopefully shall reunite with my family.

I kept crying and tears never dried in my eyes. One day, while I was going for a walk pushing my daughter's stroller, I was stopped by a lady friend who condoled me on my father's death. She also added that when the radios of the Arab countries spoke about my dear father's death, she was surprised to see me at that time wearing a red dress going out for a walk with my daughter in the second hand stroller (that dress I have grabbed from my closet in Jaffa). The news which that friend have heard were not said to me and I was in complete darkness, going out for walks and behaving as natural as anything until I discovered it later by my self. Naturally, I have explained to that good friend that I was never notified and that my husband and the rest of the individuals in the house did that for my sake lest I might collapse.

We remained living in the same house performing my daily duties towards my family and assisting the old lady in the kitchen.

One day, I woke up early as usual, fed my child and my husband ate breakfast. My husband left home for an errand and myself got dressed as well as my daughter. Rima at that time turned eleven months. She was able to stand against the bed and play with her toys. On that day I have combed her hair differently and had tied it with a red ribbon to the back, thus keeping it away from falling on her eyes. She was a real pretty and healthy child. She was everything to me. I left her standing against our bed playing with some of her simple toys and went to the kitchen to help the old lady with the cooking which as far as I can remember was stuffed zukini and stuffed eggplant. As I have mentioned before, Nawal the mentally disabled thirteen years old girl was living with us. This girl is a non stop runner, running from one room to another, even to the bathrooms. I have kept an eye on this girl since we met. Also, her grandmother watched her whereabouts every second in the house and kept calling her by saying "Nawal where are you" and Nawal answers "Tata I am here followed by a funny tone" and that was our daily routine keeping our ears wide open to realize where she was. If the atmosphere is quiet, her grandmother and myself knew that she was doing something mischievous and immediately we run after her to stop the damages she plans to do and so on and so forth. On that same day while I was in the kitchen doing the stuffing of the zucchini, there was a moment of silence immediately followed by my daughter's loud cry. I rushed to my bedroom to see Rima falling on her back on the ground. Nawal had grabbed her pony tail and pulled her back to the ground and ran away. With my dirty hands I lifted up my distraught crying daughter, hugged her to calm her down. When I looked at her tearful eyes, I saw crossed blue eyes!!! and not the usual beautiful coloured eyes. I lost my nerves and said O God, eviction from our homes, migration, loosing my dear father, and over and above to hurt my baby by causing the crossed eyes?? This is too much and unbearable. I collapsed with my baby in my arms. The old lady did her utmost to support me and while doing that my husband came back, knew what had taken place and immediately held his daughter and rushed her to the doctor. The doctor's name was Dr. Muneer Waheed. He and his family were our friends. Dr. Waheed said that there was no cure except that her mother meaning me is to follow the opposite way when I feed Rima or bathing or reading stories or singing or playing thus training the eyes to go back to their original positions. This requires a lot of work, patience and perseverance. This what my husband said to me when he came back with Rima in his arms asking me to forget everything and just take care of our daughter. Also the old lady advised me to take care of myself being devastated and frail and to take care of my daughter and never ever think to help in the housework. Your daughter is your priority she said.

Nawal was reprimanded and was told what she did to the child. You could see sadness on her face, but after a while she went back to her abnormal routine. Her two uncles have decided to keep her in mental hospital in Egypt, but their mother and her aunt rejected the idea.

Now I am with my daughter all day long following the doctor's instructions. It took more than a month of training to rectify the eyes. I did my utmost to save the innocent child. I did the training with tears in my eyes all the time, while smiling or singing or reading stories or feeding or bathing etc.. It was a painful, difficult and sad experience, but successful at the end whereas the eyes got back to the normal position. I thanked God the Almighty and have decided to move out and not to stay a single minute.

In 1949, an American organization named "Quakers" was sent by the UN to assist the Palestinian refugees in Gaza, Lebanon, Jordan, and Syria where the Palestinians had taken refuge though many had migrated to Iraq, Egypt, Libya, US and other foreign countries. The goal of the Quakers was to provide the Palestinian refugees with food, lodging (tents), medical facilities and other things pertaining to the daily life of that destitute nation and we were one of them. While looking for a place to live as I have mentioned before, we met by chance a person who was just employed by the Quakers to run their projects. After briefing him about our situation, the latter offered my husband a job in a medical facility to work as a dispenser. Also knowing that we were looking for a place to live, he suggested that his family consisting of a wife and two kids will be glad that we share the house and live together, thus assisting us financially. To make the story brief, we thanked the Zacharia family for their wonderful hospitality and moved to a house with the Khashadourians in the Rimal Quarter in Gaza.

1949 – I'm with Yousef & Lucy Kashadourian, their children
Victor & Jessica and my Daughter Rima

We had one bed room and shared kitchen and bath. They had two bedrooms, one for the parents and the other for the kids. The wife named Lucy was so sweet and kind. She welcomed us warmly, and we lived together as sisters, cooking together and sharing all facilities in that house. They had a boy and a girl aged eight and six. We lived together for almost two years.

Before I go any further, it is worth to mention that when we first moved to live with that family, my husband was without work for almost six months. It took the Quakers a while to establish projects in the various refugee camps and employ Palestinian workers who were in dire need of money. My husband was employed in a small medical facility containing a doctor, three nurses and a small pharmacy not far away from where we lived. It was just a walking distance which, as a matter of fact, was easy for my husband to go to work to and fro. Living together with that nice family was great and peaceful. Their lovable children were highly raised. The mother was a pretty lady with a kind heart. The husband was decent and joyful and never accepted to take our share in the rent of the house saying that he considered us as one of his family and that the low monthly salary of my husband is to be kept for our own use specially that we had at that time two kids. Our second child was born in that shared house in our bedroom assisted by a midwife. Lucy, the mother of the kids, took care of me. During labor, she was with the midwife in our room calming me down and helping the midwife re-the delivery, providing warm water etc.. until our boy was born whom we named Ramez. Every one was happy to see the new born, born far away from home and family. My feelings were a mixture of happiness, sadness and loneliness to see myself having a new born in a strange environment with a vague future. That moment reminded me of my home and the scattered family and the death of my loving father whom I used to be proud of. Those flashes were interrupted by the crying of the infant telling me that I am here, feed me and take care of me mom! And I did take care of that lovely boy as well as the daughter despite confronting difficult circumstances.

After delivery Lucy took care of me and the children. She was better than a sister to me, so kind, so helpful and comforting. Our daily life proceeded smoothly until one day Mr. Khashadourian said to me and husband that his wife is sick, and that I should not be close to her for the sake of myself and the kids. He also said that she had tuberculosis and that he plans to get a nurse to serve her. I remember I used to hear her coughing on and off at night. I was really scared and tried to distance myself from her as much as I could. I loved that lady and tried my best not to hurt her feelings until the hired caregiver arrived and took care of her not allowing her to leave her bed. Lucy used to call me to see me and the kids, but in a gentle way I behaved to the contrary.

After a short period, her health deteriorated, and in a spur of the moment and without our knowledge she was moved out of the house and flown via the UN caribou to Lebanon. She was hospitalized in a private hospital for tuberculosis patients. She was secluded from husband and children. In order to be close to Lucy, the mother, Mr. Khashadurian and children also moved to Lebanon. The father was offered a good job by the UN in Beirut. As for Lucy she stayed in hospital until she passed on. It was really so sad to hear later about her death and to loose that fine lady and a dear friend.

Now we had no other alternative except to look for a cheap rent place to live, taking into consideration that we never had paid rent while with the Khashadourians and many thanks for their kind help. After searching here and there, we were told about a small one bedroom apartment owned by the Sayegh's family in the Rimal area as well. The owner is a church man who gives religious speeches every Sunday day at the Greek Orthodox church sited in Gaza, in the downtown vicinity. The family is warm, hospitable and religious and my husband and I felt so comfortable and admired the whole atmosphere and had agreed to rent the small apartment attached to their big house. We agreed on the rent and moved immediately to that site. The apartment consists of a small bedroom, a small kitchen and a small living room. The toilet was in a small room with a shower. The construction was simple and primitive. The apartment had two tiny verandas of course on the first floor (it is a one floor accommodation).

We moved our furniture which consisted of one bed (given to us by Im Khalil) and another child's bed given to us by the Shawwa family who were our neighbours while we were living with the Khashos. Our daughter used that bed and the newborn shared our bed. Thanks to both families for their kind contribution towards a displaced family.

1958 – The family at home in Gaza

Now we are at the new apartment with the two beds, our clothes and few kitchen utensils. We had no furniture since we were sharing the Khashos well furnished home. Again thanks to that wonderful family the Khashadourians. Our financial situation was still tight. The monthly pay check of my husband could barely cover rent and food. But we needed some furniture to use for our daily life with two kids. I remember while visiting my husband at work, I saw a number of empty wooden boxes (used for shipping medical supplies) kept in a small room to be taken away. I asked my husband if I can be provided with ten boxes to be sent to our apartment. He accepted the idea and the boxes were sent. I immediately used the four medium size boxes by putting one over the other thus getting four shelves to keep in our daily necessities.

One of the wooden boxes was used to keep the baby boy's clothes after making small partitions inside ie. one for diapers, one for napkins etc. Four wooden legs were fixed to that box to keep it off the ground. It was done by my husband. As for the remaining five wooden boxes I kept them in the kitchen using each one for different kitchen utensils, dishes and other kitchen wear. Now after organizing all the wooden boxes, I bought cretin coloured material to use it as curtains to cover the various boxes. Since I have the knowledge how to sew, I did the job by hand stitch without a sewing machine. As for the furnishing of the small living room, I got another five boxes on which I have placed a used mattress covering it by the same coloured cheap cretin cloth. In order to make a coffee table, I brought three wooden boxes and put them on the floor side by side and covered it with a simple plain coloured table cloth. The apartment looked simple and neat with the wooden boxes furniture! I had so many compliments from friends who visited me and it is unbelievable to mention that people who knew me at that time still talk at present about the apartment and about my creativity.

It was the first time since we migrated from Jaffa that I got back my freedom as the lady of the house keeping the apartment neat and tidy though furnished with wooden boxes .It was a mistake not to take pictures of that simple lodge. My two kids were well taken after. They were healthy, beautiful with red cheeks. Mothers in the neighborhood used to ask me re- the daily food menu I gave to my kids and I remember how I assisted and taught mothers in this regard.

For the first time in Gaza a pre-school for kids has been opened by a young lady named Lucy Waheed. The preschool was in her own home, accepting kids from two years of age and above. Knowing very well this good family, we thought of enrolling our daughter who was only two years in that kindergarten. There was a certain fee to be paid monthly, but I forgot how much it was. In order to get Rima to that location which was not far from where we lived, we hired a housekeeper and her name was Amneh. The latter took Rima to the preschool daily with the exception of weekends. She used to carry her from home to school and vice versa. Amneh is a Palestinian refugee who migrated with her family from their home village named Hiribia to Gaza. Maids at that time were very cheap because of poverty. We liked Amneh who was clean and honest. She liked the kids and the kids liked her. The apartment in which we were living is part of the owner's house. Only a closed door separates us. The Sayegh's (the owners) were a wonderful family with sons and daughters. I was so glad to be nearby this Christian family who were so fond of my children. Rima and Ramez were both two pretty healthy kids. When Rima is taken by Amneh to the pre-school, Ramez is left by me. After feeding him at noon vegetable soup with a spoon (and which he would not open his mouth to eat unless Amneh does images and sounds with his toys) I hear Mimi one of the neighbour's daughters calling me if it is time for her to pick Ramez.

They know when Ramez eats via the commotion they hear during the feeding hour.

I took care of my adorable children and home. I began to know neighbours living nearby. We reciprocated visits. The political atmosphere was quiet. Egypt was ruling Gaza at that time and the Quakers as mentioned before were looking after the Palestinian refugee's welfare. We were satisfied with two kids and never thought of having another child because of our tight financial situation. The pay check which my husband got each month could barely cover the various expenses ie. rent, food, milk and clothing etc.. But to our surprise I discovered that I was pregnant and decided to terminate the pregnancy from the beginning. I consulted my neighbour Mrs. Sayegh who was the wife of the owner and the latter advised me not to do anything lest I hurt myself for being young. My Husband and I were determined not to have another child because of our vague and tragic situation. None the less I proceeded with my decision and tried to lift a heavy stone which I found in the garden of our neighbours. Also, tried to lift a jar filled with water, also got into the bedroom of my neighbour and tried to move a wooden cupboard full of clothes. While going through all that and my neighbour was yelling at me to stop it. However, all what I have went through had no effect. My husband consulted the doctor, who works with him in the small clinic, and the doctor recommended special pills which I took but again it did not work and I remained pregnant despite all efforts. Accepting what God had planned for us, I began to prepare gradually what is needed for the new born. The owners of the apartment introduced me to a well known capable midwife whom me and my husband have agreed that she will be my midwife. Her name was

Sadiqa Sayegh. I would like to mention here that there was only one hospital in Gaza named the Baptist hospital and it was not as yet ready to receive pregnant women for deliveries. However, I had a routine exam by my midwife and everything was going on well health wise for baby and me. Connections between Gaza and the outside world including Jordan where my family resides were prohibited. Therefore I had no communications whatsoever with my family. Now that I am in my ninth month, I began to feel signs of labor. It was a hot day in August 1951 when I called my midwife and on the same day in the afternoon Randa our daughter was born. Now having three kids it was a full time job. The three kids and us were in the same one bed room, Rima in her bed, Ramez as well in his own bed and Randa the baby on our bed between her father and myself. It reminds me one early morning I woke up and I saw Ramez standing in his bed clinging with his small hands to the surrounded bars of his wooden bed watching me if I am awake so that I can give him his bottle of milk and change diapers. He was one year old when our baby Randa was born. Being exhausted all through the night breast feeding Randa, I tried to ignore him and hid my face under the cover. When trying myself to see what he was doing, we both had an eye contact and he smiled thinking that I will get up and feed him etc…but I hid my head again and he kept watching my reactions until the milk man showed up calling me with a loud voice to open the door and get the fresh cow's milk. Ramez, the blond pretty boy screams with happiness saying (mama, mama, haleeeb haleeb aja haleeb) meaning that I should get up and give him his bottle of milk and haleeb means milk and aja means came. He was a darling and of course I got up put the milk on the stove to boil and during that period I changed his diapers as well as for Rima and afterwards gave both their bottles of milk which they both grab and enjoyed drinking.

Raising three kids was a full job. Every day I used to prepare the food menu for daughter and son each day different than the other. As for the baby it was a different menu in addition to breast feeding. I loved my kids and they were everything to me. As time went by, I became more and more oriented people wise and of course through the Sayeghs and the Zakharias. I started to acclimatize to the situation but still yearning to meet my family, mother sisters and brother. After staying few years in the same apartment, we thought of baptizing the three kids. The owner welcomed the idea and offered his house for the baptism occasion. A number of friends were invited and the Greek Orthodox priest baptized the three children and the God Father was Mr. Sayegh the owner of the house. The Sayegh family took care of everything. Thanks to their kindness. They were wonderful people and considered them as my family.

The Sayegh family needed the small apartment for their son, and therefore we were obliged to look for another cheap apartment in the same area, and we did. It was close to where we were and the rent was cheap. We stayed in that apartment for almost two years. I got introduced to new families, thus getting more and more friends. The owners were friendly and hospitable. One day, and in a polite manner, the owner asked us if we can vacate the small apartment (since he needed it for his family) and of course we did, and we moved to another apartment in the same area. The apartment was small and the rent was reasonable. We stayed in that apartment for one year and again the owner asked us to vacate since he needed it for his increasing family. He also assisted us by finding another apartment. We did move to that apartment and have stayed for a while. I got introduced to other neighbours in the environment, but do not forget how hard I worked to get organized when moving three times from one place to another with three kids.

As mentioned above, the Gaza strip was ruled by the Egyptians. In 1952 the United Nations relief and works agency for Palestinian refugees replaced the Quakers and established offices in the various Arab countries including the Gaza strip. The offices were used for administration, employment and for running the various humanitarian services extended to the Palestinian refugees in the various ten camps, such services and more, are still being rendered to the Palestinian refugees up to this date and I think that this operation will last for ever as long as the Israeli and Arab conflict exists. In March 1953 I was offered a job to work as a secretary to the Director of UNRWA Operations but rejected the offer because my kids were still young and it was hard for me to leave them with an untrained housekeeper. But my husband (who in principle was against employment) encouraged me and asked me to accept the offer since we were experiencing a tight budget. To make the story short, we got a good housekeeper to take care of the children and I was allowed to leave work two hours a day to check on my kids. Transportation was provided by the Agency.

I began work and it was from 7.30am to 2.30pm with Saturdays and Sundays off. The Boss was an American middle aged man. He was married with children. He was nice and considerate. My job was interesting but hard at the same time. To run the office of the director needs efficiency and concentration. I liked what I was doing, and tried my best to achieve what was required. In return I got a good salary as a start. I worked for two years during which period we rented a decent house, furnished it with the items needed, thus retaining gradually our standard of living. Our children were happy and content. They were provided with the toys they like, and got used to live with a housekeeper and sometimes two in the house.

Working in my UNRWA office in Gaza

In the month of December 1956, while I was typing an urgent letter to the director, we were interrupted by the fearful roaring of war planes so low over us speeding like lightening. On that day, I remember all employees were asked to leave work and go home. It was a surprise to the whole world to hear that the three allies Britain, France and Israel attacked with their war planes the Egyptian armed forces in the Sinai desert. The invasion was a response to Jamal Abdul Naser the president of Egypt for his declaration to nationalize Suez Canal and to end the British control over the canal. It was a blow to the British, since the canal was the main artery of the British Empire and the treaty signed in the year 1954 between the two parties had ended.

1966 - A meeting with my boss in my office

We stayed home without work for a while until UNRWA called all its employees to go back to work. During that period, the Israeli army occupied the Gaza strip. The Egyptians were expelled and driven out of the strip, but after a short period the United States Of America who was not consulted re-the invasion ordered the Israeli army to withdraw and to be replaced by the Egyptian Government authority. Also the United Nations emergency forces (UNEF) joined the Interim government as peace makers. During that period, the Gaza residents and the Palestinian refugees who migrated to Gaza from the nearby villages and towns got a sort of stability and peace during that era. The Egyptian administration to the strip was coordinated by UNRWA in all aspects ie. Education, distribution of rations, accommodation etc. As for the subject of education, the Gaza strip followed the Egyptian curriculum and it was implemented in all schools. After Tawjihi (end of the secondary cycle) the graduates who attained high grades, were allowed to join the Egyptian universities in Egypt. The university graduates, either Palestinian refugees or Gaza citizens owe the Egyptian Government million of thanks for the great help offered. With the cooperation of UNRWA, the Egyptian administration in the Gaza strip lasted for almost 27 years. There was peace and tranquility during their era.

During that period our fourth daughter was born. I was a working mom. Naturally, I had a good reliable housekeeper at home who took care of the children. I worked hard to compromise between work and home. The children were well cared after. I was enjoying my job and getting a good salary thus getting what is needed for a good standard of living of course with the income of my husband.

Having only one son, my mother kept nagging that we should get a brother to our son and it was a joy to all the family when the new born was a boy, thus having three daughters and two sons.

We lived in the rented house for almost ten years. It was a beautiful villa surrounded partly by fruit trees. One of the fruit trees was so high that it needed a ladder to reach it, and I remember our son Ramez who was eleven years made a wooden ladder long enough to reach the fruits. The fruit is named (Jummeize) or sycamore a delicious healthy fruit. It is from the family of fig trees. While still living there, I remember we owned a car and was parked in the small garage included in the house. We had a dog named Rocky who guarded

47

the whole place. How the car was purchased is mentioned here under.

One day we were told that the house we were living in has been sold to another owner and the new owner needed the house for his grown up children. It was so disappointing to all of us to leave that independent home. The new owners offered us a lump sum of money to meet the new high rent of another apartment and not a house. We agreed and we moved to an apartment in a newly built building in the Rimal area. Just before the move, it was always on our mind to buy a car but not an expensive car.

1960 – The Zakharia family at our house in Gaza

The Deputy Director of the UNRWA operations decided to quit his job and go back to the US. He owned an Austin car and wanted to sell it and the bid was cheap. A number of employees applied to buy the car. Mr Euwart, the owner, in order to be just he made a ruffle and my husband won the car .The car was parked in the car port of the house. Of course my husband was glad to re-own a private car, since as he said that he owned a private car since he was seventeen years of age. The children enjoyed their rides with their Dad.

We remained for a while in the old house, until everything was finalized paper wise to move to the new apartment.

The family at church on Palm Sunday

It is worth to mention here that the wife of the new owner Rabi'ah Shurrab called to congratulate me for finding the house clean and never expected to find it in an excellent condition after ten long years of usage with five children.

We picked the flat on the second floor. The apartment consisted of two bedrooms, a formal sitting room, a spacious living and dining room, an entre and a big kitchen. Also one full bath and half a bath. It was an up-to-date apartment sited in a good environment. We were very satisfied with the new move specially that it was in a convenient spot. As for our beloved dog Rocky, we were not allowed to move him to our new residence because as alleged that he will cause disturbances to the building community. My husband gave him to a friend far away from where we lived, but still he walked back to the old house and was brought to the place where we moved in. We tried to convince the owner to keep him behind the building to guard the area but our request was turned down supported by the new tenants!! It was so devastating to us, and the dog was moved to a very far area and had never returned.

Now being in the new modern apartment with five children, we began to organize it room by room adding new furniture, décors, drapes etc...The veranda to the west of the apartment was furnished with white steel chairs, table and a blue umbrella. What is interesting to mention here that I bought clay jars, two of a big size while the six remaining were smaller. I painted all the jars with a yellow colour and wrote on each one the names of the family including our small dog Ringo.

1970s – The family tree

My husband helped me with the drilling and hanged the big jars on top and the six jars below. It looked like a family tree whereas later when the children got married we included small jars for the grandchildren with their names on each jar. There was a variety of flowers in the veranda which my husband had planted and it looked awesome.

We got so many compliments by our visiting friends. The names of our five children were Arabic names all starting with the alphabet "R". The names are Rema, Ramez, Randa, Raghda and Rajaii. Also our indoor small dog named Ringo. The idea of the alphabet "R" goes initially to a friend of my husband who came to visit us at Regent Hotel when on honey moon as mentioned previously and did not find us. His name was Ramez. I liked the name and kept it for myself to name our first child after him. Our first born child was a girl and we named her Reem (Rima) thus naming the second born Ramez and continued to name the rest of the children with the alphabet "R".

In that apartment we got a new very good housekeeper who took care of the children and house keeping the apartment while both of us were at work. Our children who attended pre-school, kindergarten, elementary and secondary government schools were healthy and intelligent. The curriculum they experienced was Egyptian all through their scholastic years.

During that period of time I was promoted to a number of positions with UNRWA. I worked for the Medical and Education Departments and my final position was Women' Program Officer in the Department of Welfare. The latter position was the most interesting job since it rendered vital services to the Palestinian women in the various refugee camps. The goal of the five programs monitored by me was to train the refugee women and girls, through the projects they experienced, to become bread earners, thus assisting themselves and their families financially I loved my job and was so much devoted to it. The success I have achieved in this field was rewarded by various reassessments and upgrading of my post. I have contributed great organizational skill, enthusiasm and hard work to serve the girls and women in their respective refugee camp. I remained in this position till my early retirement in the year 1987.

Now back to our new apartment which we were so busy to organize and to get oriented with the new environment and neighbours; also change of schools for the children was part of the work. However we managed to implement what is necessary and then gradually accomplished the remaining chores. Also we were lucky to be allowed by the owner to keep two cages of poultry (chickens and pigeons) in the back yard of the building. They were moved from the old house to the new. My husband was so happy to have them being his favourite hobby.

As mentioned above we had a good housekeeper named Im Rafeek who used to report daily before our departure to work. During that period we all get up, help the children to dress up for school, eat breakfast which included a cup of milk mixed with a fresh egg from our poultry take a sandwich and go to school.(Rima, our oldest daughter was the milk and egg provider every

A meeting at my office with my boss and my daughter Randa

morning). At that time Rajaii was the only child still attending a kindergarten, while the rest were at elementary and preparatory cycle. Rajaii, our youngest boy was cute and healthy. He did not like sometimes to go to his Kindergarten. When the bus comes to pick him up, he ushers to the driver to go away saying that his tummy hurts and that he does not feel well to go to school. To the contrary, he takes off his brown uniform with the white collar, opens his blue plastic food box which includes a sandwich, fruit and candies and eats it all. Im Rafeek calls me at work complaining that she has a lot to do at home and had no time to watch him etc. I speak to Rajaii and calm Im Rafeek down, and Rajaii promises not to repeat it, but it was repeated all through his kindergarten years.

Also it reminds me once about our son Ramez who was still in the elementary cycle and said one early morning" I do not want to go to school today, and is it a must that I should go to school every day, everyday? (I still remember his small index finger pointed at us alerting us of his intentions and saying (I went yesterday and the day before and that is enough) and of course his father and myself explained to him the importance of education for his future life.

Time flies so fast. Our five children have grown up doing so well at their respective schools. Rima our eldest daughter was an exemplary student always attaining high marks. During her preparatory cycle, she managed to finish the curriculum of three preparatory classes in one year (the Egyptian Department of Education allowed that procedure only to the outstanding students but not anymore during the Egyptian era), and I remember because of her distinguished high grades, she was awarded a number of gifts given to her by the Egyptian Military Governor of Gaza through the educational ceremonies held by the Department of Education in this regard. Rima reciprocated by thanking the Governor and the audience through her short speech which was prepared by herself and mom's assistance.

Continuing successfully with her studies all through the secondary cycle, and choosing the literary section on the scientific, our daughter attained the highest grades in her Tawjeehia. Before proceeding, I would like to mention here that her choice to select the literal cycle was due to my mom's remarks saying that quote why should you graduate as an Engineer or doctor etc.

wasting seven years of your life studying? You are a pretty girl and to graduate literally suits your personality much more than the Scientific unquote. This followed a long discussion and finally Rima was convinced and enrolled in the literal section. The second day when her Principal heard about it, she called me on the phone at work telling me (If Rima Zacharia is not enrolled in the scientific section, whom do you think can do that?), and she was really upset. However, as mentioned above, Rima finished her Tawjihi with honour.

Now and after graduation her father and I began to think where Rima should go to attain her university degree. She had applied through the department of education to join the Egyptian universities, and the subject she selected was political science. She got the acceptance, but her father and I declined the offer for several reasons.

With my daughter Rima at the BCW, Beirut

Once I read a brochure about (Beirut College for Women) in Lebanon, and came to know that students with high grades are awarded scholarships. I discussed the subject with husband and daughter and the three of us agreed to inquire about the enrollment of our daughter in that college. I began to correspond Dr. Francis Grey, the President of the college mentioning in details everything about our financial status and the high grades our daughter had attained all though her school years from KG to Tawjeehia. In return I got answers from the President asking me to answer a number of queries and forms to fill etc. and which I did adding the information that we are Palestinian refugees residing at present in Gaza. It took a while correspondence-wise between the college and me, until finally the president of the college invited me and daughter to fly to Beirut for an interview. Being a senior staff member with UNRWA, I was allowed and my daughter to board the UN caribou and flew to Beirut. We were met there by Dr. Francis Grey, the President of the College who asked her secretary to bring the file of Mrs Zacharia (all my letters were kept in a special file). We discussed several points and finally interviewed my daughter. She was so much impressed by Rima's personality and knowledgeable answers and said that Rima is accepted at the BCW. (Freshman) Rima at that time was only sixteen years old.

We flew back to Gaza and my husband was so glad to hear the good news. We started purchasing all the college necessities including clothes, stationery, suit cases etc.

It was in the year 1965 when our daughter flew back to Beirut to join the first semester at the BCW. Being accepted (Freshman) she was awarded a scholarship but (not full) because her father and my self were employees with monthly pay cheques.

At the embroidery shop in Gaza with one of my employees

Therefore arrangements were made with my employer to transfer a monthly amount of dollars (I forgot the exact amount) from my monthly salary to the guardian assigned to my daughter in Beirut. The amount transferred covers cost of books and other miscellaneous and personal expenses.

While at college, it took our daughter a while to acclimatize with the new situation especially language wise, but I kept encouraging her and pushing her forward. Being an intelligent and industrious all her life, Rima became a straight (A) student well known amongst her colleagues and of course to the President of the BCW. The word {congratulations} was all the time written on her grades' sheet which we used to receive each semester from the College.

The rest of our children were still in government schools in Gaza. Both my husband and I were working as usual with the UNRWA organization.

My UN car in the Gaza Strip. January 1986

Everything went on smoothly in the Gaza strip under the Egyptian rule headed by the administrative military Governor General.

The political situation had never been stable in the region especially between the neighboring Arab countries and Israel. During June 1967 Israel declared war against those countries including Egypt. The Israeli war planes destroyed completely the Egyptian air force and on 6th of June 1967 the Israeli forces captured the Gaza Strip, and led the Egyptian Governor General into captivity. The war was known as the six days war.

After a long fearful situation of shooting for almost a week, night and day it reminds me when we were obliged to rush to the first floor to hide with our children to avoid the bullets, since a number of them penetrated the closed window on the second floor, and landed on the buffet causing a big hole and another bullet hitting a shelf in the dining room. Also it reminds me as well of Ramez who was so much terrified and hid under his bed in the children's bed room!! Capturing, and imposing curfews all over the Gaza strip, lasted for almost two months whereas and during that period the curfew sometimes was lifted to allow the residents to buy their groceries and the timing was only two hours , but was extended later for more than two hours. The inhabitants including ourselves experienced fear and sufferings all through the period of the invasion until the occupation stabilized and gradually the curfews were lifted and imposed only at night from 7pm to 6am, notifying the residents of the Gaza strip through loud-speakers re-new orders or announcements.

Now being again under the Israeli occupation, the residents of Gaza as well as the Palestinian refugees

Giving a lecture on the work I was performing with UNRWA

59

living in the various camps which UNRWA had provided became under the rule of a new Israeli Government headed by an Israeli Governor. Back to work resumed cautiously by the inhabitants.

After the occupation the Israeli Government allowed the Gaza people to travel to the West Bank as well as Israel after a long period of closure. In order to travel a person should obtain a travel permit from the Israeli authorities who sometimes took two weeks or a month. The new policy was to allow the residents of the Gaza Strip as well as those of the West Bank to find jobs abroad, thus rendering an outlet for workers (men and women to earn their own living). My brother and family were living in Ramallah. Also my sister in law and family were living there as well. Our third daughter named Raghda who did not get along well with the English teacher at her school, asked to be transferred to another school in Gaza. Raghda was a good student doing very well in class and adhering to her wish she accepted to be transferred to a boarding school in Ramallah. The name of the school was Rahibat Al Wardia. Other students from Gaza were encouraged as well to send their daughters to that school mostly because of the unstable situation in Gaza. Also our son Ramez who was supposed to finish his third secondary class (Tawjihi) in Gaza was obliged to leave Gaza in an illegal manner to Amman Jordan. Ramez, as far as I can remember, with the help of his father hired an old truck with other passengers and paid the driver a good amount of money, just to transport him and others through illegal routes to reach Amman. He and others hid under old mattresses with other miscellaneous goods in the back of the truck in order not to be caught by the Israeli army who, eventually, searched the truck, but Ramez and others held their breaths until the search was over and were not traced by the army. Apparently God was with them and thank you God. The old truck proceeded to Jordan through rough unpaved roads until they reached Amman. It was the most dangerous and tiring trip that our dear son had went through, only for the sake of education. There he stayed first with my sister and family who migrated from Jaffa in 1948 and then spent a whole scholastic year with a relative who took care of him and assisted by enrolling Ramez in a Jordanian secondary school which was near by the house in which they both were living.

Age wise there is only one year between Ramez and Randa, and due to the unwanted Israeli occupation to the Gaza strip by the residents, the political situation especially school wise was very much unusual. Throwing of stones by students at Israeli tanks and soldiers was seen daily. Shooting of rubber bullets by the army towards people is heard everywhere killing and injuring a number of young men nearly every day. The residents of Gaza strip struggled hard against the

Meeting my daughter Randa who was coming back home from
college at Lydda Airport, Tel Aviv

occupation and the whole situation became critical
and unsafe. Our second daughter Randa who was
supposed to finish third secondary (Tawjihi) in Gaza,
and due to the political instability education wise, we
decided to transfer her to a secondary school in
Ramallah named Al-Kullieh Al-Ahliah. Randa lived at
her aunt's house (My husband's sister) because her
school was a day school. The curriculum in the West
Bank was Jordanian and also under the Israeli
occupation.

Our youngest son Rajaii, who was still in the
elementary cycle stayed with us until his graduation. As
for Ramez, and after finishing his secondary education
in Amman, where he attained a high grade (Tawjihi
Science stream) returned home to join Beirzeit College

in the West Bank. Only Freshman and Sophomore was functioning in that College including dormitories for the students to live in and of course food was served. Ramez was admitted and graduated attaining high grades, as usual.

After her graduation from the Al-Kullieh Al-Ahllieh in Ramallah, Randa joined the same college and met with her brother who graduated before her.

In order to attain his BSc degree, and after doing the necessary paper work, our son was accepted at the American University in Beirut.

He headed to Amman to fly to Lebanon, but unfortunately he was stranded there due to the outburst

My son Rajai's first birthday

of the Black September (a fierceful savage fight between the PLO and the Jordanian army which had lasted for almost a month.) At that time, I had two sisters living in Amman, and Ramez stayed in the apartment of my oldest sister.

It was so detrimental to our son and the rest of the inhabitants to survive. They suffered from lack of food especially bread and water. Hundreds were killed or burnt or injured without any first aid or medical assistance. Corpses could be seen all over as well as the injured including men women and children asking for help. My sister who was a widower living with her three daughters asked our son to fetch for water despite the deadly atmosphere.

He was thirsty as well and by his going out to get water was almost shot by the snipers, but God saved him because I was praying daily asking God to protect him and God answered my prayers and saved him. Thank you God.

When cease fire was imposed, and the airport opened, our son was lucky to find a plane going to Beirut. He was met there by his close friends who took good care of him. He was destitute hungry and unaware of what was going on. With the help of his colleagues he was admitted to the A.U.B. During that period and through my work, I kept in touch with the Red Cross in Gaza, and asked them to look for my son. The Red Cross gave us the good tidings that our son is alive and that he is already in Beirut. It is worth mentioning here that during the month of the Black September in the year 1979, Jamal Abdul Nasser, the President of Egypt passed away. President Nasser negotiated with King

Hussein to stop the fighting between the PLO army and that of the Jordanian. His death was a shock to the region. The Arab world mourned him specially his people since he was a strong honest leader on whom the Arabs in general and the Palestinians in particular had the full trust in him to restore their confiscated land, freedom and dignity. His funeral in Egypt was above description. The whole Arab world mourned him including myself. It was so emotional and detrimental to loose a great leader

Now that our five children are still getting their education at different places, Rima, the oldest daughter who was studying at B.C.W. got engaged, married, and flew with her husband to Doha, Qatar. Due to the occupation of the Gaza Strip by Israel (the Six-Day War) in the year 1967, we were unable to proceed to Lebanon to attend her wedding. The family of the bridegroom had planned to hold a big wedding in Gaza, but because of the serious political circumstances, all the arrangements set were cancelled.

As for our son Ramez, who was studying at the AUB, had graduated and headed to the United States for further studies. He joined the University of Southern California to attain his master degree in Engineering and in the year 1976; the school of engineering have conferred to Ramez the degree of Master of Science in Electrical Engineering. After graduation he planned to return home, to work in the Gulf region, but fortunately, he got a job with a company in the US who assisted in granting our son the American Citizenship. With this citizenship, we were able to be granted our own and reunited with our children in the US. Thanks to our son.

Ramez got a number of high positions with various companies all through his work in the United States.

As for Randa our second daughter, who was at Birzeit College, had graduated and attained her sophomore degree, where she was later admitted to Beirut College for Women in Beirut. Raghda, our third daughter who finished her secondary education, was as well admitted to the same college in Lebanon. Our youngest son was still at school in Gaza.

Me and a guest at the veranda of our house in Gaza

Life in Gaza strolled peacefully but cautiously during the occupation of the Israeli government to the Gaza Strip. The boarders between Gaza and Israel were opened, to enable Palestinian refugees and Gaza residents to work in Israel. The inhabitants being exhausted after a long weary period of war, fear and poverty, were in dire need of a job to earn their living.

The nearby Arab countries in the region, had their doors widely opened to employ university graduates and others to work in Kuwait, Qatar , Saudi Arabia etc...The economical situation started to improve and people began to breath the essence of a stable life. The United Nations relief and works agency continued offering various services to the Palestinian refugees in the Gaza strip in coordination with the local government. Both my husband and I were still working and everything went on smoothly for quite a good period of time. Our son Rajaii, who was doing so well at school, reached his final year of secondary education which is named Tawjihi. The curriculum as mentioned above was Egyptian. Our son worked hard all through that year in order to attain a high grade. I still picture him with our little dog (Ringo) solving mathematics, geometry, algebra etc..in the living room, and as he said once, that Ringo was his companion and incentive to concentrate on what he was doing. We raised Ringo for twelve years. He was our pet, especially when all our children left the house.

Our son sat for the Tawjihi exam, science stream, and attained high marks. He was accepted at the Jordan University in the school of Science which he had rejected and asked to be transferred to the School of Engineering, though in the back of his mind he wanted to fly to the United States to join his brother who already graduated and got a job. It was the opinion of our oldest son to have his brother with him in the United States to pursue his university education, but my husband and myself were against the principle of allowing Rajaii at the age of eighteen to go a different world! We had long discussions with our sons, whereas we came to a conclusion that if the University of Jordan transfers Rajaii to the school of Engineering the latter will stay in

67

the same university. Therefore, I got the approval to absent myself for one week from work and proceeded to Amman via the Jordan Bridge which was an unpleasant trip to go through. I arrived at my daughter's house and that night, I called the phone number of the residence of the President of the university and I did not expect that the President himself would answer. I introduced myself to him and asked for an appointment to meet him in his Office. He agreed and said that I can meet him at ten am the next day.

Everyone, especially my son in law were amazed and never expected to hear what was accomplished. To meet the President of the University, to discuss with him the subject of transfer was unbelievable. But it happened.

At ten am I was at the office of the President while Rajaii waited for me on the first floor of the building. I was welcomed by his secretary who offered me a cup of tea, and then called to meet His Excellency. After long strenuous discussions re- the transfer from the school of Science to the School of Engineering, the President approved it after consultation with the University Members of Trustees. The President handed me the transfer instructions to give to the University Registrar, who in turn got it typed and gave it to my son to countersign it by the members of the Board of Trustees, each in his respective office. Rajaii, knowing that he already was transferred to the School of Engineering, yet he could not believe what was going on.

Thanks to the President of the Jordan University for his kind assistance for the transfer as well as for keeping the academic seat of Rajaii till the end of the university scholastic year in case Rajaii is prevented to leave the

Gaza strip because of the occupation, and thanks as well to Rajaii's mom who did what she could to convince the President to approve the transfer, but mainly because of the high grades which Rajaii had attained.

Despite all the efforts made to keep Rajaii in the school of Engineering, still he insisted to join his brother in the United States. Also his brother encouraged him to join the US universities and had sent him the ticket to fly. My husband and I tried all means to stop him from flying to an extent that we hid his Passport, but finally all our endeavors have failed. With the help of his brother, Rajaii joined the school of engineering at San Diego state university. It was so sad to miss our youngest son who was our companion especially in the tragic political atmosphere of the Gaza Strip. Rajaii was needed morally to both of us. We cried when he departed. He left Gaza and never came back. We met again in the United States.

Now back to both of us, husband and I, we both kept working and living of course in Gaza. My husband retired and got his retirement benefits which were spent on children's' education and I continued working. The situation in Gaza became very tense and critical. The second intifada began especially when it was agreed that the PLO government is to be replaced by the Israeli occupation. Throwing of stones on Israeli army increased as well as shootings. It was so risky to drive the UN car in the various refugee camps to monitor my work or even go to my office. Demonstrations by the residents were almost seen every day and to make it short, my husband and myself began thinking of leaving the region and reunite with the two sons in the US. We have paid our dues towards our children, and own no properties in the Gaza Strip being except the furniture we own in our homey apartment. I loved my job and it was hard for me to quit, but unwillingly, I asked for an early retirement and it was in the year 1987. The Director of the UNRWA operations rejected the resignation and asked me to stay until they find someone to step in my shoes. Also he called me in person and convinced me to stay and gave me two weeks to think it over. Again I discussed it with my husband and our decision was that we should leave and I finally resigned.

Business trip to Vienna. September, 1979

The Director of UNRWA Operations awarded me with a certificate which says:" Mrs Nuha Zakharia has worked for the United Nations Relief and Works Agency for Palestine Refugees in the near East since the 2nd of April 1953. During the first ten years of her work Mrs Zakharia was employed first in an educational and then in a secretarial capacity. On 26/9/1963 she was appointed as Assistant Field Welfare Officer (female) a post which she held till her early retirement on 2nd September 1987. During her time in this post she established and developed successfully a series of women's activities throughout the Gaza Strip which provided a model and a target to other of the Agency fields. The success she achieved was rewarded by various reassessments and upgrading of her post. Mrs Zakharia contributed great organizational skills, enthusiasm and hard work in the 1960's and 1970's to developing the sewing centers and women's activities centers through out the Gaza Strip and to establishing the Agency's Embroidery Shop in the Gaza town. She has laid a good foundation for the expected expansion under her successor of the Agency's programme for women, and is to be congratulated for her hard work in the past" signed by B.H.G.Mills, Director of UNRWA Operations Gaza and UNRWA representative in Egypt

It was so hard for me to quit my job to an extent that I have regretted the decision taken. It took a while to get over it until one day we decided to leave the area leaving behind us our home and go on a trip to England and the USA. First we visited England where my daughter and family live and then headed to the United States where our sons reside.

We spent almost two months in the United States visiting our three children going around with suit cases which was rather uncomfortable to both of us. Also we stayed for a while at my sister in-law's house, until one day we decided to rent a one bedroom apartment which we finally did. As for the furniture needed, we rented a number of items from a company named "Brooks" and began to discover if we both could acclimatize and stay

71

in the US. The apartment we rented was small compared to the house we were living in while in Gaza. Also language, customs and traditions was strange to us and had felt lonely and rather isolated.

We decided to go back despite the unstable political situation. We kept the apartment but returned all the rented furniture to the respective company. We flew back to Gaza and resided in our still existing rented furnished apartment. The political situation was tense since our arrival to Gaza. It coincided with the return of the Chairman of the PLO to the Gaza Strip. It was in the year 1993 when the agreement of the Oslo accords was signed recognizing the chairman of the PLO as the representative of the Palestinians and that Israel has the right to exist. Consequently, in the year 1994, the PLO Chairman with his associates came back to Gaza. It reminds me of that night when the Israelis withdrew and the PLO took over. There was a continuous gun fire all through the night and all residents were scared unknowing what was going on. We stayed in Gaza for a short period and had decided finally to sell the furniture, keeping only few items incase we might return if stability takes place. Because of the vague situation we flew back to the United States, bought new furniture and resided in the already rented apartment the location in which I am still renting. In the year 1995 my husband passed away leaving me by my self in the said apartment.

The five children are married. Rima in England, Ramez and Rajaii in SanDiego, Randa in Kansas and Raghda in Rohnert Park.

In the year 2006, I started thinking of writing the story of my life since my expulsion from Jaffa up to this date. I am oriented somehow re -the computer technique, and based on that, my children provided me with a good computer. Being a stenographer and typist (a course which I had after graduation at the British Institute in Jaffa), helped me to use the key board by typing with ten fingers. I still remember typing and my speed is still good as well as my Pitman's shorthand.

I began typing my story in the year 2007, taking it very easy intuition wise. I have planned to finish it early before 2009.

CONCLUSION

It is sad to end my story by saying that since the expulsion of the Palestinians from their homes in Palestine in the year 1948 up to this date, the tragic conflict between the Palestinians and the Israelis has been going on for the past half century. Hatred, vengeance, imprisonment, kidnapping, torturing, massacres, killing, air raids and last but not least the latest complete eradication of a population in the Gaza Strip through air raids, mortar shells, tanks and infantry.

It was a criminal and heinous act implemented by the Israelis and condemned by the whole world. There shall be no peace in the Holy Land unless the Palestinians are given back their rights and their country which was confiscated illegally by Israel, thus

Evicting the Palestinians from their homes and stranding them all over the world. Palestine is still occupied, the conflict between the two parties is still going on and the future is unknown!!!

RECAPITULATION RE- THE CONFLICT

Palestinians are Muslims and Christians fighting side by side to recover the land that was usurped from them by the Israelis. The Germans may have committed the holocaust, but the weaker Palestinians are paying the price with their lives, their homes, their lands their future and that of their children. They are akin to the French Resistance Movement during WW1who tried to expel the occupying Germans from their lands. The French efforts ceased with the end of the war, but the war in Palestine still goes on and on for the past 63 years. Somehow, the rise of the Islamic movement promulgated by the Al-Qaeda leader and his cohorts has distracted the attention of the world from the plight of the Palestinians, and the Jewish propaganda has done an outstanding job in confusing the minds of the world and particularly the Americans by equating the Palestinian cause with the Islamic movement.

Made in the USA
Middletown, DE
09 February 2022